Ideal
School Supply
Company

S0-CFC-404
Grades 1-3
ID 7457

Math Discoveries
ABOUT
Counting & Numbers

Shirley Hoogeboom

Math Discoveries About Counting and Numbers

Grades 1-3

Shirley Hoogeboom is an author, curriculum developer, and editor for Ideal School Supply Company. She has taught grades one through four and preschool students with special needs. During 20 years in educational publishing, Shirley has written and edited materials for a computer-managed instructional program, and has authored or coauthored over 100 books and sets of games and activities for math, reading, and language arts. She has also conducted workshops for teachers in the use of math manipulatives.

Shirley holds a bachelor of arts degree in Education from Calvin College where she earned her Michigan State Teaching Credential. She completed further studies in education at the University of Minnesota and earned her California Teaching Credential at California State University, Hayward.

Cover illustration by Frank Cirocco
Illustrations by Donna Reynolds
Graphic Design by Annelise Palouda
Project Manager: Nancy Tseng

© 1995 Ideal School Supply Company
Oak Lawn, Illinois 60453
Printed in U.S.A.
ISBN: 1-56451-125-1

1 2 3 4 5 6 7 8 9 10. 9 7 6 5 4 3 2 1

Contents

Math Discoveries About Counting and Numbers, Grades 1-3 • © Ideal School Supply Company

Notes to the Teacher

This book is part of a series of books of math activities for primary students. The books are:

Math Discoveries With Attribute Blocks, Grades 1-3

Math Discoveries With Base Ten Blocks, Grades 1-3

Math Discoveries With Calculators, Grades 1-3

Math Discoveries About Counting and Numbers, Grades 1-3

Math Discoveries With Geoboards, Grades K-1

Math Discoveries With Geoboards, Grades 2-3

Math Discoveries With LacerLinks,™ *Grades K-1*

Math Discoveries With LacerLinks,™ *Grades 2-3*

Math Discoveries With Money, Grades 1-3

Math Discoveries With Pattern Blocks, Grades K-1

Math Discoveries With Pattern Blocks, Grades 2-3

Math Discoveries With Tangrams, Grades K-1

Math Discoveries With Tangrams, Grades 2-3

Math Discoveries About Time, Grades 1-3

These books are designed to help your students build mathematical concepts and understandings through hands-on activities with concrete models. The activities engage students in "doing mathematics," which is emphasized in the National Council of Teachers of Mathematics (NCTM) Standards. The models invite students to explore, represent, solve problems, construct, discuss, investigate, describe, and predict.

The activities encourage students to work together in pairs and small groups. When the children manipulate physical models, then use their own language to explain their thinking, they build deeper mathematical understandings and develop their communication skills. The physical models serve as a focus for communication, even among students who do not share a primary language.

Attribute Blocks, geoboards, Pattern Blocks, and tangrams all allow students to develop spatial sense and to explore geometry informally. Base Ten Blocks, the hundred number board, number tiles, and a number line provide models of our number system, and LacerLinks can be used to model numbers, operations, and spatial patterns. Play coins and bills are models of our system of currency and exchange, and clocks are models for measuring time. Calculators can be used for exploring number concepts, patterns, operations, and as a problem-solving tool.

Each book presents 40 reproducible one-page activities for students, extension activities, two investigations for more in-depth explorations, a game, and student awards. Sample problem solutions are also included.

Introduction to *Math Discoveries About Counting and Numbers*

The activities in this book require a number line that shows the numbers 0 through 25; number charts that show the numbers 0 through 99 and 1 through 100; and number tiles 0 through 100. These materials provide excellent models for children to use to explore our base ten number system.

Number lines and charts help children see relationships between numbers and talk about them. They also help students explore number patterns, discover strategies for mental computation, and develop meanings for the operations of addition, subtraction, and multiplication. Number tiles help children order numbers and investigate even and odd numbers. All three manipulatives can be used with these problem-solving strategies: act out the problem, and use a picture or diagram.

The activities in this book are designed to help students develop the math skills and understandings articulated in the NCTM Standards.

NCTM Standards Math Skills and Understandings	Activities That Develop These Skills and Understandings
Construct number meanings, using physical materials and real-world experiences	Activities 1-40; Investigations 1 and 2
Develop number sense	Activities 1-40; Investigations 1 and 2
Relate counting and place-value concepts	Activities 1-5, 11-20; Investigations 1 and 2; Game
Recognize, describe, and extend patterns	Activities 16-25, 31-40
Explore number relationships	Activities 6-10, 16-25, 31-40; Investigations 1 and 2; Game
Explore using variables and open sentences to express relationships	Activities 31-35
Develop operation sense; model addition, subtraction, and multiplication	Activities 11-30; Game
Explore mental computation techniques	Activities 11-30; Game
Solve problems and puzzles; use problem-solving strategies	Activities 1-40; Investigations 1 and 2
Develop the language of mathematics	Activities 1-40; Investigations 1 and 2
Collect, organize, and display data	Investigations 1 and 2

Using *Math Discoveries About Counting and Numbers*

Contents

This book contains a series of 40 activities, divided into eight sections. Each section presents five activities that are similar, giving students the opportunity to use and develop particular skills. An extension activity is provided for each section.

The book also includes a game and two longer, more open-ended activities called *investigations*. The game gives children practice in addition and subtraction, and helps them develop strategies for mental computation. The investigations give children the opportunity to extend and deepen their learning and to apply what they have learned to solving a problem.

Solutions are provided for the activities. In many cases, the solutions given are only samples of the many solutions possible. Blackline masters for number charts, a number line, and student awards are also included.

Suggestions for Classroom Use

The activities are sequenced according to level of difficulty within each section and from section to section throughout the book. If you find that an activity or section is too challenging for your students, or not challenging enough, you can modify it to meet their needs. You may want to encourage the students to do the extension activity after each section. These extensions encourage further exploration of the ideas in the main activities and often ask the children to share their discoveries.

These activities can be used by students working in pairs or individually in a learning center or in small cooperative learning groups. Working together encourages students to talk about their thinking and their discoveries. It is beneficial for students to articulate their thinking and to hear how others may have solved the same problem in a different way. Encourage the children to share their ideas with other pairs of students, with other small groups, or with the whole class.

Materials Needed

It is recommended that each student or pair of students have available a number line showing numbers 0 through 25, a number chart and number tiles showing the numbers 0 through 100, and a pencil for doing the activities. You can make copies of the activities and extensions for each student or pair of students, or you can place copies in a learning center. You may want to provide copies of the 0-99 chart, the 1-100 chart, and the number line on pages x-xi. The two parts of the number line must be cut out and taped together. The numbers in the charts can be cut apart and used as number tiles.

Have your students record on the activity sheets. If your students are not able to record on paper, you can have them show you their work with the number tiles, or on the number line or number chart.

For the Trail Twister game, players will need two different-colored crayons or markers, a copy of the game rules (page 49), and one or two sets of the game cards (page 50). It is recommended that you back the game cards with heavy paper before you cut them apart.

Introducing the Activities

If your students are not familiar with the number line, number tiles, and number charts, give them free time to just look at them and find numbers on them. This free exploration will give them a chance to satisfy their curiosity regarding the materials before they begin using them to solve problems. You may want to talk about storage and management of the materials at this time.

If your students are just beginning to learn about using number lines and number charts, you might introduce them through a couple of group activities:

• Have the children work together in pairs. Give each pair a number line that shows the numbers 0 through 25. Have one partner begin at zero, then move to 1, to 2, and so on up to 25. Let the other partner say the numbers as the child moves across the number line. Then talk about what number would come next on the number line. Encourage the children to talk about what a number line is and why it has an arrow to the right of the number 25. Help them understand that the number line could go on indefinitely.

Say: **Start at number 2 on your number line. Count on 1. What number do you end on?** Let the children answer together. Then say: **Start at number 8. Count back 1. What number do you end on?** After the children answer, encourage the partners to take turns telling what number to start on

and how much to count on or count back.

• Give each pair of students a 1-100 chart and a pencil. Ask the children to think about how a number chart is like a number line and how it is different. Encourage the children to give their ideas.

Say: **Circle number 2 on your number chart. Count on 2. Circle the number you end on. Count on 2. Circle the number you end on. Keep counting on in the same way, all the way to 100.** Give the children time to complete their skip counting by twos. Then ask the partners to look at the numbers they have circled and talk together about the pattern they see.

Do the same activity again, having the children put an X on the number 10, count on by 10, and put an X on every number they end on. Then ask the partners to look for a pattern in the numbers they marked. Have two pairs of partners talk together about the pattern they see.

When you are ready to introduce the activities in a section, lead the students through the first activity of the section. Point out the instructions about what the students will need and about recording. Tell the children to use the fronts and backs of the activity sheets for recording.

Following are brief descriptions of the activities, extensions, investigations, and game.

• **Activities 1-5:** Ordering numbers 0 through 25 from lowest to highest and from highest to lowest. Children take a given set of number tiles and put them in order from lowest to highest or from highest to lowest. They solve puzzles by ordering a group of numbers and filling in missing numbers. They use a number line to check their work. In the Extension, partners put number tiles 0-25 in a bag, then take turns drawing out a handful and ordering the numbers. They use a number line to check.

- **Activities 6-10: Identifying mystery numbers, using clues and a number line.** Children read clues about a number or group of numbers. The clues focus on the relationships between numbers, and use such language as *more than, greater than, less than, higher than, lower than, between, closer to, before, after*. The children use logical thinking and the number line to find the mystery numbers. Students also write their own clues about mystery numbers. In the Extension, partners write clues about mystery numbers and let friends find the numbers.

- **Activities 11-15: Counting on and counting back on a number line; adding and subtracting on the number line.** Students start at given numbers, then count on or count back to find an end number. They solve puzzles in which the end number is given, but the other numbers are unknown. In activity 15, the students write number sentences for the problems in which they count on and count back. In the Extension, partners write their own puzzles and let friends solve them.

- **Activities 16-20: Counting on and counting back by ones, tens, and multiples of 10 on a number chart; exploring patterns that result.** Students start at given numbers, then count on or count back by 1, 10, or multiples of 10 to find an end number. They find the patterns that result from "1 less than and 1

more than," and "10 less than and 10 more than." These patterns become visible on the number chart. In activities 19 and 20, they use the patterns to help them add and subtract two-digit numbers quickly on the number chart. These activities help children discover and develop strategies for fast mental computation. In the Extension, partners take turns marking two numbers on a 1-100 chart, and quickly computing the difference between them.

- **Activities 21-25: Exploring number patterns on the number chart: even and odd numbers; and multiples of 5, 10, and 11.** Students mark given numbers on a number chart, then look for a pattern in those numbers. They follow the pattern and mark the remaining numbers on the chart. They look at the ones' digits, or tens' and ones' digits, in the numbers, and write about the pattern. Then they use the pattern to identify mystery numbers. In the Extension, partners write their own clues about mystery numbers and let other students identify the numbers.

- **Activities 26-30: Making arrays with number tiles; writing multiplication sentences that describe the arrays.** Students take a given set of number tiles and arrange the tiles in rows. They write multiplication sentences to describe the arrays; for example, "1 row of 4 = 4; 2 rows of 4 = 8." Then they use the same set of number tiles to solve multiplication puzzles. Finally, they write their own puzzles about the number tiles. In the Extension, partners use the number tiles to explore prime numbers in an informal way. They find numbers that make even rows in only two ways; for example, 5 rows of 1 and 1 row of 5.

- **Activities 31-35: Identifying the rules of "function machine" robots; using the rule to predict; expressing the rule in a number sentence.** Pairs of Numbers In and Numbers Out are given in a table. Students look for a pattern in the way the numbers in each pair are related, then use that pattern to complete other pairs of numbers. The children then express that pattern as a generalized rule; for example, Number In + 3 = Number Out. Encourage students to replace words by symbols; for example, replace Number In by the letter *I*, and Number Out by the letter *O*. In the Extension, partners create their own Robot's Rules puzzles and exchange them with other students. The students talk together about how they solved the puzzles.

- **Activities 36-40: Solving problems and puzzles, using number tiles, number charts, and a number line.** Students solve a variety of problems and puzzles about numbers and number relationships. The problems are presented in stories and also in numerical form. The children use whatever they think will help them solve a problem: the number line, number tiles, or number chart. In the Extension, partners create a variety of number puzzles. They let other pairs of partners solve the puzzles and share their thinking while solving them.

- **Investigation 1: Number Lines Around Us.** Students might enjoy this investigation after they have completed Activities 1-20. This activity is designed to help children discover how they use lines of numbers in their daily lives. They begin by looking around them in the classroom. They find a variety of lines of numbers—some straight, as on rulers and yardsticks; and some curved, as on watches, clocks, and dials. Then the students look for lines of numbers outside of the classroom. They describe what they find, and tell how the lines of numbers are used. Finally, the children choose a way to organize and display their work for everyone to see.

- **Investigation 2: Create a Calendar.** Students might enjoy this investigation after they have completed Activities 21-40. The children begin this project by comparing a calendar and a number chart to find out how they are alike and different. Then they write a story about a land in which the calendar is different from their own calendar. They choose the number of days in a week, weeks in a month, and months in a year for their story land, and make the calendar. Finally, they figure out how old they would be if they lived there.

- **Game: *Trail Twister*.** This game is designed for two players, but it could be adapted for more players. It is designed to give players additional practice in adding, subtracting, and using clues to find numbers on a number chart. Each player chooses a number in the first row of a 1-100 chart and marks it with his or her color. Then the players take turns drawing game cards, following the instructions given, and marking the numbers they end on. The first player to have connected numbers from the first row of the chart to the last row is the winner.

ix

1	2	3	4	5	6	7	8	9	10
11	12	13	14	15	16	17	18	19	20
21	22	23	24	25	26	27	28	29	30
31	32	33	34	35	36	37	38	39	40
41	42	43	44	45	46	47	48	49	50
51	52	53	54	55	56	57	58	59	60
61	62	63	64	65	66	67	68	69	70
71	72	73	74	75	76	77	78	79	80
81	82	83	84	85	86	87	88	89	90
91	92	93	94	95	96	97	98	99	100

 - - - - - - - - - - - - - - - - Cut Here - - - - - - - - - - - - - - - -

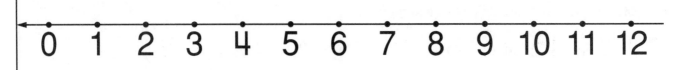

0 1 2 3 4 5 6 7 8 9 10 11 12

x

0	1	2	3	4	5	6	7	8	9
10	11	12	13	14	15	16	17	18	19
20	21	22	23	24	25	26	27	28	29
30	31	32	33	34	35	36	37	38	39
40	41	42	43	44	45	46	47	48	49
50	51	52	53	54	55	56	57	58	59
60	61	62	63	64	65	66	67	68	69
70	71	72	73	74	75	76	77	78	79
80	81	82	83	84	85	86	87	88	89
90	91	92	93	94	95	96	97	98	99

- Cut Here - - - - - - - - - - - - - - - - - -

13 14 15 16 17 18 19 20 21 22 23 24 25

Math Discoveries About Counting and Numbers, Grades 1-3 • © Ideal School Supply Company

Sample Solutions

There are many solutions possible for some of the problems. The solutions shown for the problems marked with an * are only samples.

1. A 1, 2, 3, 4, 5, 6, 7, 8, 9, 10
   B 3, 4, 5, 6, 7, 8, 9, 10, 11, 12
   C 7, 8, 9, 10, 11, 12, 13, 14, 15, 16

2. A 0, 1, 2, 3, 4, 5, 6, 7, 8, 9
   B 11, 12, 13, 14, 15, 16, 17, 18, 19, 20
   C 17, 18, 19, 20, 21, 22, 23, 24, 25, 26

3. A 9, 8, 7, 6, 5, 4, 3, 2, 1, 0
   B 16, 15, 14, 13, 12, 11, 10, 9, 8, 7
   C 24, 23, 22, 21, 20, 19, 18, 17, 16, 15

4. A 20, 19, 18, 17, 16, 15, 14, 13, 12, 11
   B 25, 24, 23, 22, 21, 20, 19, 18, 17, 16
   C 19, 18, 17, 16, 15, 14, 13, 12, 11, 10

5. A 0, 1, 5, 6, 8, 9, 12, 15, 16, 17
   B 6, 7, 9, 11, 13, 14, 18, 20, 23, 25
  *C 4, 6, 7, 9, 12, 15, 16, 17, 20, 25

Note: Answers for G and H will vary on pp 6-10.

6. A 13 B 10 C 5 D 12 E 7 F 10

7. A 9 B 15 C 4 D 20 E 17 F 15

8. A 8 B 14 C 18 D 20 E 24 F 21

9. A 9, 10, 11 B 16, 17, 18, 19 C 22, 23, 24
   D 19, 20 E 18, 19 F 16, 17, 18, 19

10. A 2 B 13 C 19 D 11 E 8 F 20

11. A 11 B 11 C 6 D 6 E 8 F 10 G 8
    H 3

12. A 12 B 12 C 12 D 11 E 13 F 13
   *G 7,7 *H 3,8

13. A 7 B 1 C 7 D 7 E 2 F 5 G 12 H 9

14. A 7 B 10 C 8 D 10 E 20 F 10
   *G 18, 19 *H 15, 7

15. A 13: 10 + 3 = 13 B 15: 12 + 3 = 15
    C 7: 16 - 9 = 7 D 3: 10 - 7 = 3
    E, F Answers will vary.

16. A 4 B 7 C 26 D 39
   *E Count on by 1, end on the number to the right of the start number; count back by 1, end on the number to the left.
    F 17, 18, 19, 20 G 34, 35, 36, 37, 38

17. A 32 B 28 C 6 D 40

*E Count on by 10, end on the number below the start number; count back by 10, end on the number above it.

F	1	2		G	18	19
	11	12			28	29
	21	22			38	39
	31	32			48	49
	41	42			58	59

18. A 26 B 39 C 55 D 68

F	54	55	56		G	9	10
	64	65	66			19	20
	74	75	76			29	30
	84	85	86			39	40
						49	50

19. A 30 B 23 C 98 D 22 E 63 - 12 = 51
    F 21 + 21 = 42 G, H Answers will vary.

20. A 40, 2; 81 B 20, 1; 49 C 10, 5; 9
    D 30, 6; 80 E 35 + 16 = 51 F 65 - 15 = 50
    G, H Answers will vary.

21. A 0, 2, 4, 6, 8, 10, 12, 14, 16, 18, 20, 22,
       24, 26, 28, 30, 32, 34, 36, 38, 40, 42,
       44, 46, 48, 50, 52, 54, 56, 58, 60, 62,
       64, 66, 68, 70, 72, 74, 76, 78, 80, 82,
       84, 86, 88, 90, 92, 94, 96, 98
   *B The ones' digit in an even number is 0, 2, 4, 6, or 8.
    C 24, 26, 28, 30 D 26, 28, 30, 32, 34

22. A 1, 3, 5, 7, 9, 11, 13, 15, 17, 19, 21, 23, 25, 27,
       29, 31, 33, 35, 37, 39, 41, 43, 45, 47, 49, 51,
       53, 55, 57, 59, 61, 63, 65, 67, 69, 71, 73, 75,
       77, 79, 81, 83, 85, 87, 89, 91, 93, 95, 97, 99
   *B The ones' digit in an odd number is 1, 3, 5, 7, or 9.
    C 45, 47, 49 D 55, 57

23. A 0, 5, 10, 15, 20, 25, 30, 35, 40, 45, 50, 55,
       60, 65, 70, 75, 80, 85, 90, 95
   *B The ones' digit is 0 or 5.
    C 25 D 50

24. A 10, 20, 30, 40, 50, 60, 70, 80, 90, 100
   *B The ones' digit is 0; the tens' digits increase by 1.
   *C 110, 120, 130, 140, 150

25. A 11, 22, 33, 44, 55, 66, 77, 88, 99

B The tens' digit and ones' digit are the same.
*C 22 *D 77

Note: Answers for C will vary on pp 26-35.

26. A 1 row of 2 = 2; 2 rows of 2 = 4;
   3 rows of 2 = 6; 4 rows of 2 = 8;
   5 rows of 2 = 10; 6 rows of 2 = 12
   B 3 rows of 4 = 12; 2 rows of 6 = 12

27. A 1 row of 4 = 4; 2 rows of 4 = 8;
   3 rows of 4 = 12; 4 rows of 4 = 16
   B 2 rows of 8 = 16; 8 rows of 2 = 16

28. A 1 row of 3 = 3; 2 rows of 3 = 6;
   3 rows of 3 = 9; 4 rows of 3 = 12;
   5 rows of 3 = 15; 6 rows of 3 = 18
   B 3 rows of 6 = 18; 2 rows of 9 = 18

29. A 1 row of 6 = 6; 2 rows of 6 = 12;
   3 rows of 6 = 18; 4 rows of 6 = 24
   B 3 rows of 8 = 24; 2 rows of 12 = 24

30. A 1 row of 5 = 5; 2 rows of 5 = 10;
   3 rows of 5 = 15; 4 rows of 5 = 20;
   5 rows of 5 = 25; 6 rows of 5 = 30
   B 3 rows of 10 = 30; 5 rows of 6 = 30

31. A

In	Out
8	10
5	7

Number In + 2 = Number Out

   B

In	Out
10	15
14	19

Number In + 5 = Number Out

32. A

In	Out
10	7
12	9

Number In - 3 = Number Out

   B

In	Out
9	4
12	7

Number In - 5 = Number Out

33. A

In	Out
5	10
6	12

Number In × 2 = Number Out

   B

In	Out
2	6
7	21

Number In × 3 = Number Out

34. A

In	Out
18	10
24	16

Number In - 8 = Number Out

B

In	Out
8	24
3	9

Number In × 3 = Number Out

35. A

In	Out
12	22
9	19
18	28

Number In +10 = Number Out

   B

In	Out
61	41
75	55
59	39

Number In - 20 = Number Out

36. A 35 *B 41
   C
   D

37. A 3 blocks
   B
   C

   *D 36

38. A 15, 20, 25, 30, 35, 40, 45, 50
   *B

   C 25 D 21 blocks

39. A 18; Number of Seeds Planted × 2 =
   Number of Plants
   B 12 + 5 = 7 more than 10
   25 + 50 = 100 - 25
   89 - 40 = 1 less than 50
   50 - 25 = 10 + 10 + 5
   *C

   D 100

40. A 7 × 4 = 28; 28 third-graders
   B 48 + 51
   C 50
   D 5, 15, 25, 35, 45, 55, 65, 75, 85, 95, 50,
   51, 52, 53, 54, 56, 57, 58, 59

Math Discoveries About Counting and Numbers, Grades 1-3 • © Ideal School Supply Company

Awards

Fantastic!

_____
name

You are fantastic because _____
_____

Brilliant!   **Wow!**   **Outstanding!**

Signed _____ Date _____

_____
name

is a Numbers Expert!

You are a Numbers Expert because _____
_____

Super Work!   **Prize Winner!**   **Top Dog!**

Signed _____ Date _____

Use ▶ Number Tiles, Number Line, and a pencil.

✏️ Record your work.

Put the number tiles in order.
Go from lowest to highest.

A. Take number tiles 4, 6, 3, 5, 2, 7, 1, 10, 8, 9.

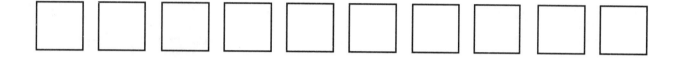

B. Take number tiles 12, 8, 6, 7, 5, 4, 3, 9, 11, 10.

C. Take number tiles 16, 10, 11, 8, 7, 9, 12, 14.
Put them in order.
Find the missing numbers.

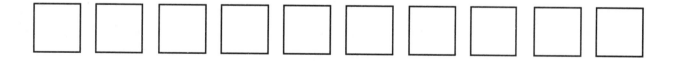

D. Use the number line to check your answers.

Math Discoveries About Counting and Numbers, Grades 1-3 • © Ideal School Supply Company

Use▶ Number Tiles, Number Line, and a pencil.

Record your work.

Put the number tiles in order.
Go from lowest to highest.

A. Take number tiles 0, 6, 3, 5, 2, 7, 1, 4, 8, 9.

B. Take number tiles 20, 18, 16, 17, 15, 14, 13, 19, 11, 12.

C. Take number tiles 17, 22, 26, 24, 20.
   Put them in order.
   Find the missing numbers.

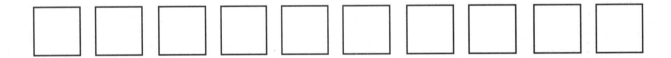

D. Use the number line to check your answers.

2

Use ▶ Number Tiles, Number Line, and a pencil.

Record your work.

Put the number tiles in order.
Go from highest to lowest.

A. Take number tiles 6, 4, 0, 9, 2, 7, 1, 3, 8, 5.

B. Take number tiles 7, 12, 15, 13, 16, 14, 10, 9, 11, 8.

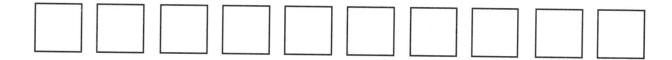

C. Take number tiles 17, 20, 15, 19, 24.
Put them in order.
Find the missing numbers.

D. Use the number line to check your answers.

4

Put the number tiles in order.
Go from highest to lowest.

A. Take number tiles 14, 17, 19, 11, 15, 16, 20, 18, 12, 13.

B. Take number tiles 16, 25, 17, 24, 22, 20, 21, 23, 18, 19.

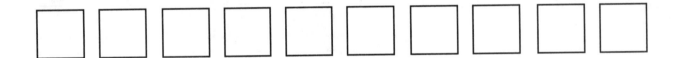

C. Take number tiles 19, 15, 10, 11.
    Put them in order.
    Find the missing numbers.

D. Use the number line to check your answers.

Put the number tiles in order.
Go from lowest to highest.

A. Take number tiles 17, 5, 0, 12, 8, 15, 1, 6, 9, 16.

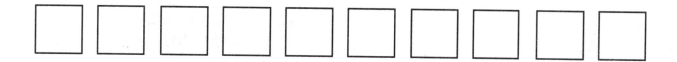

B. Take number tiles 7, 23, 11, 14, 6, 20, 25, 18, 9, 13.

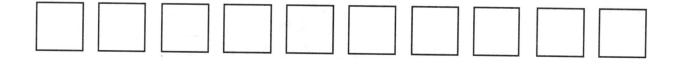

C. Take number tiles 4 and 25.
   Find eight numbers that go between them.

D. Use the number line to check your answers.

Name _____

Use ▶ Number Line and a pencil.

 Record your work.

Find the mystery numbers.

A. I am between 12 and 14.

   What number am I?_____

B. I am 1 more than 9.

   What number am I?_____

C. I am before 6.
   I am after 4.

   What number am I?_____

D. I am more than 11.
   I am less than 13.

   What number am I?_____

E. I am 1 more than 6.

   What number am I?_____

F. I am 1 less than 11.

   What number am I?_____

Write your own clues for mystery numbers.

G. I am _____

   _____

   _____

   What number am I?_____

H. I am _____

   _____

   _____

   What number am I?_____

Find the mystery numbers.

A. I am 1 less than 10.

What number am I?_____

B. I am 1 more than 14.

What number am I?_____

C. I am higher than 3.
   I am lower than 5.

What number am I?_____

D. I am more than 19.
   I am less than 21.

What number am I?_____

E. I am 1 more than 16.

What number am I?_____

F. I am 1 less than 16.

What number am I?_____

Write your own clues for mystery numbers.

G. I am _____

_____

_____

What number am I?_____

H. I am _____

_____

_____

What number am I?_____

Use ▶ Number Line and a pencil.

 Record your work.

Find the mystery numbers.

A. I am between 6 and 9.
I am not 7.

What number am I?_____

B. I am between 10 and 15.
I am after 13.

What number am I?_____

C. I am between 16 and 19.
I am not 17.

What number am I?_____

D. I am between 19 and 22.
I am not 21.

What number am I?_____

E. I am between 22 and 25.
I am not 23.

What number am I?_____

F. I am greater than 20.
I am less than 22.

What number am I?_____

Write your own clues for mystery numbers.

G. I am _____

_____

_____

What number am I?_____

H. I am _____

_____

_____

What number am I?_____

Math Discoveries About Counting and Numbers, Grades 1-3 • © Ideal School Supply Company

9

Use ▶ Number Line and a pencil.

 Record your work.

Find the mystery numbers.

A. We are less than 12.
We are greater than 8.

What numbers are we?

_____

B. We are greater than 15.
We are less than 20.

What numbers are we?

_____

C. We are after 21.
We are before 25.

What numbers are we?

_____

D. We are greater than 18.
We are less than 21.

What numbers are we?

_____

E. We are higher than 17.
We are lower than 20.

What numbers are we?

_____

F. We are between 15 and 20.

What numbers are we?

_____

Write your own clues for mystery numbers.

G. We are _____

_____

What numbers are we?

_____

H. We are _____

_____

What numbers are we?

_____

Name _____

Use ▶ Number Line and a pencil.

 Record your work.

Find the mystery numbers.

A. I am between 0 and 3.
   I am closer to 3 than to 0.

   What number am I?_____

B. I am between 12 and 15.
   I am closer to 12 than to 15.

   What number am I?_____

C. I am between 17 and 20.
   I am closer to 20 than to 17.

   What number am I?_____

D. I am between 9 and 12.
   I am closer to 12 than to 9.

   What number am I?_____

E. I am between 7 and 10.
   I am closer to 7 than to 10.

   What number am I?_____

F. I am between 18 and 21.
   I am closer to 21 than to 18.

   What number am I?_____

Write your own clues for mystery numbers.

G. I am _____

   _____

   _____

   What number am I?_____

H. I am _____

   _____

   _____

   What number am I?_____

Math Discoveries About Counting and Numbers, Grades 1-3 • © Ideal School Supply Company

Use ▶ Number Line and a pencil.

 Record your work.

Count on to find each end number.

A. Start at 8.
   Count on 3.

   End number?_____

B. Start at 3.
   Count on 8.

   End number?_____

C. Start at 2.
   Count on 4.

   End number?_____

D. Start at 3.
   Count on 3.

   End number?_____

E. Start at 5.
   Count on 3.

   End number?_____

F. Start at 5.
   Count on 5.

   End number?_____

Solve the puzzles.

G. Start at _____.

   Count on ___4___.

   End number?___12___.

H. Start at _____.

   Count on ___7___.

   End number?___10___.

0   1   2   3   4   5

Count on to find each end number.

A. Start at 7.
   Count on 5.

   End number?_____

B. Start at 6.
   Count on 6.

   End number?_____

C. Start at 8.
   Count on 4.

   End number?_____

D. Start at 6.
   Count on 5.

   End number?_____

E. Start at 4.
   Count on 9.

   End number?_____

F. Start at 9.
   Count on 4.

   End number?_____

Fill in the numbers.

G. Start at _____.

   Count on _____.

   End number?__14__.

H. Start at _____.

   Count on _____.

   End number?__11__.

Use ▶ Number Line and a pencil.

 Record your work.

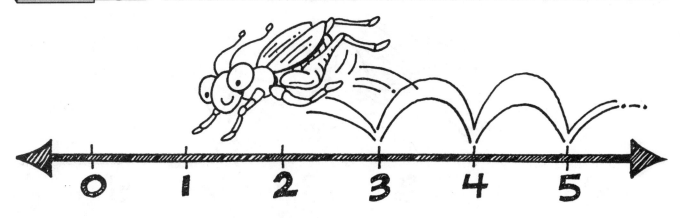

Count back to find each end number.

A. Start at 10.
   Count back 3.

   End number?_____

B. Start at 3.
   Count back 2.

   End number?_____

C. Start at 15.
   Count back 8.

   End number?_____

D. Start at 13.
   Count back 6.

   End number?_____

E. Start at 5.
   Count back 3.

   End number?_____

F. Start at 10.
   Count back 5.

   End number?_____

Fill in the numbers.

G. Start at _____.

   Count back ___3___.

   End number?___9___.

H. Start at _____.

   Count back ___8___.

   End number?___1___.

Math Discoveries About Counting and Numbers, Grades 1-3 • © Ideal School Supply Company

Name _____

Use ▶ Number Line and a pencil.

 Record your work.

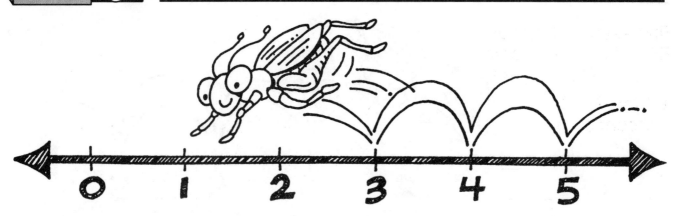

Count back to find each end number.

A. Start at 16.
   Count back 9.

   End number? _____

B. Start at 15.
   Count back 5.

   End number? _____

C. Start at 18.
   Count back 10.

   End number? _____

D. Start at 20.
   Count back 10.

   End number? _____

E. Start at 25.
   Count back 5.

   End number? _____

F. Start at 25.
   Count back 15.

   End number? _____

Fill in the numbers.

G. Start at _____.

   Count back _____.

   End number? __9__.

H. Start at _____.

   Count back _____.

   End number? __8__.

Name _____

Use ▶ Number Line and a pencil.

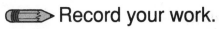 Record your work.

Find each end number.
Fill in the number sentences.

A. Start at 10.
Count on 3.

End number? _____

☐ + ☐ = ☐

B. Start at 12.
Count on 3.

End number? _____

☐ + ☐ = ☐

C. Start at 16.
Count back 9.

End number? _____

☐ − ☐ = ☐

D. Start at 10.
Count back 7.

End number? _____

☐ − ☐ = ☐

Fill in the numbers.

E. Start at _____.

Count on _____.

End number? _____

☐ + ☐ = ☐

F. Start at _____.

Count back _____.

End number? _____

☐ − ☐ = ☐

Mark the start number on your chart.
Mark the end number.

A. Start at 3.
   Count on 1.

   End number?_____

B. Start at 8.
   Count back 1.

   End number?_____

C. Start at 25.
   Count on 1.

   End number?_____

D. Start at 40
   Count back 1.

   End number?_____

E. Look at your pairs of numbers. Look for a pattern.
   Talk about the pattern with a partner.

Solve these puzzles. Don't look at your chart.
Try to fill in the missing numbers. Then use your chart to check.

F.

18		20	

G.

	35		37	

Name _____

Use ▶ 1-100 Chart and a pencil.

▬▶ Record your work.

Mark the start number on your chart.
Mark the end number.

A. Start at 22.
   Count on 10.

   End number?_____

B. Start at 38.
   Count back 10.

   End number?_____

C. Start at 16.
   Count on 10.

   End number?_____

D. Start at 30.
   Count back 10.

   End number?_____

E. Look at your pairs of numbers. Look for a pattern.
   Talk about the pattern with a partner.

Solve these puzzles. Don't look at your chart.
Try to fill in the missing numbers. Then use your chart to check.

F.

1	
	12
21	
	32
41	

G.

18	
	29
38	
	49

17

Math Discoveries About Counting and Numbers, Grades 1-3 • © Ideal School Supply Company

Name _____

Mark the start number on your chart.
Mark the end number.

A. Start at 6.
   Count on 20.

   End number?_____

B. Start at 9.
   Count on 30.

   End number?_____

C. Start at 85.
   Count back 30.

   End number?_____

D. Start at 88.
   Count back 20.

   End number?_____

E. Look at your pairs of numbers. Look for a pattern.
   Talk about the pattern with a partner.

Solve these puzzles. Don't look at your chart.
Try to fill in the missing numbers. Then use your chart to check.

F.

54		56
	85	86

G.

9	
	50

Use ▶ 1-100 Chart and a pencil.

✎▷ Record your work.

Mark the start number on your chart.
Mark the end number.

A. Start at 7.
   Count on 23.

   Hint: Count on 20, then 3.

   End number?_____

B. Start at 35.
   Count back 12.

   Hint: Count back 10, then 2.

   End number?_____

C. Start at 64.
   Count on 34.

   Hint: Count on 30, then 4.

   End number?_____

D. Start at 59.
   Count back 37.

   Hint: Count back 30, then 7.

   End number?_____

Solve these number puzzles.
Count on or count back.

E.   63 − ☐ = 51

F.   21 + ☐ = 42

Fill in the numbers you choose.

G.   ☐ − ☐ = ☐

H.   ☐ + ☐ = ☐

Mark the start number.
Mark the end number.

A. Start at 39.
   Count on 42.

   End number?_____

B. Start at 70.
   Count back 21.

   End number?_____

C. Start at 24.
   Count back 15.

   End number?_____

D. Start at 44.
   Count on 36.

   End number?_____

Solve these number puzzles.
Count on or count back.

E.   35 + ☐ = 51

F.   65 – ☐ = 50

Fill in the numbers you choose.

G.   ☐ + ☐ = ☐

H.   ☐ – ☐ = ☐

Name

Use ▶ 0-99 Chart and a pencil.

 Record your work.

21

A. Mark these numbers on your chart: 0, 2, 4, 6, 8, 10, 12, 14, 16, 18, 20.

Look for a pattern in the numbers.
Mark the other numbers that belong in the pattern.

B. The numbers you marked are called **even** numbers.

Look at the ones' digit in each number. Can you find a pattern?

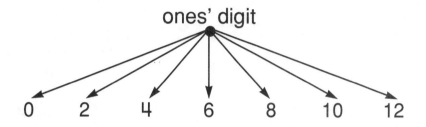

ones' digit

0   2   4   6   8   10   12

Tell about the pattern you find.

_____

_____

Solve these puzzles.

C. We are even numbers.
We are between 22 and 32.

What numbers are we?

_____

D. We are even numbers.
We are between 25 and 35.

What numbers are we?

_____

Math Discoveries About Counting and Numbers, Grades 1-3 • © Ideal School Supply Company

Name _____

Use ▶ 0-99 Chart and a pencil.

 Record your work.

A. Mark these numbers on your chart: 1, 3, 5, 7, 9, 11, 13, 15, 17, 19, 21.

Look for a pattern in the numbers.
Mark the other numbers that belong in the pattern.

B. The numbers you marked are called **odd** numbers.

Look at the ones' digit in each number. Can you find a pattern?

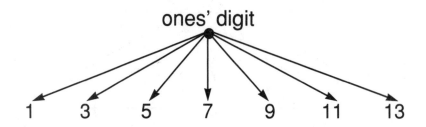

Tell about the pattern you find.

_____

_____

Solve these puzzles.

C. We are odd numbers.
We are between 44 and 50.

What numbers are we?

_____

D. We are odd numbers.
We are between 53 and 59.

What numbers are we?

_____

Name

Use ▶ 0-99 Chart and a pencil.

 Record your work.

A. Mark these numbers on your chart: 5, 10, 15, 20, 25.

Look for a pattern in the numbers.
Mark the other numbers that belong in the pattern.

B. Look at the ones' digit in each number. Can you find a pattern?

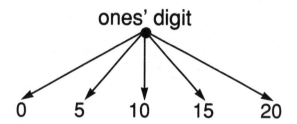

ones' digit

0   5   10   15   20

Tell about the pattern you find.

_____

_____

Solve these puzzles.

C. I am an odd number.
   I tell how much 5 nickels
   are worth.

   What number am I?

   _____

D. I am an even number.
   I tell how much 5 dimes
   are worth.

   What number am I?

   _____

Math Discoveries About Counting and Numbers, Grades 1-3 • © Ideal School Supply Company

Name _____

Use ▶ 1-100 Chart and a pencil.

 Record your work.

A. Mark these numbers on your chart: 10, 20, 30, 40.

Look for a pattern in the numbers.
Mark the other numbers that belong in the pattern.

B. Look at the tens' digit and ones' digit in each number.
Can you find a pattern?

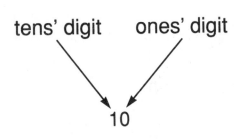

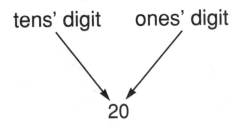

Tell about the pattern you find.

_____

_____

_____

C. What do you think the next five numbers are in the pattern?

_____, _____, _____, _____, _____,

Why do you think so?_____

Use ▶ 1-100 Chart and a pencil.

✏️▶ Record your work.

A. Mark these numbers on your chart: 11, 22, 33, 44.

Look for a pattern in the numbers.
Mark the other numbers that belong in the pattern.

B. Look at the tens' digit and ones' digit in each number.
Can you find a pattern?

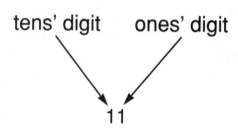

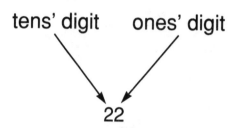

Tell about the pattern you find.

_____

_____

_____

Solve these puzzles.

C. I am an even number.
My tens' digit and ones' digit
are the same.

What number could I be?_____

D. I am an odd number.
My tens' digit and ones' digit
are the same.

What numbers could we be?_____

Math Discoveries About Counting and Numbers, Grades 1-3 • © Ideal School Supply Company

Use ▶ Number Tiles and a pencil.

 Record your work.

A. Use number tiles 1 through 12.

Put the tiles in rows of two.
Keep the numbers in order.

Show how many tiles you use for the rows.

1 row of 2 = ☐

2 rows of 2 = ☐

3 rows of 2 = ☐

4 rows of 2 = ☐

5 rows of 2 = ☐

6 rows of 2 = ☐

B. Use the same number tiles.

Solve these puzzles.

3 rows of ☐ = 21   2 rows of ☐ = 12

C. Make your own puzzles.

Use ▶ Number Tiles and a pencil.

✏️▶ Record your work.

27

A. Use number tiles 1 through 16.

Put the tiles in rows of four.
Keep the numbers in order.

Show how many tiles you use for the rows.

1 row of 4 = ☐

2 rows of 4 = ☐

3 rows of 4 = ☐

4 rows of 4 = ☐

B. Use the same number tiles.

Solve these puzzles.

2 rows of ☐ = 16   8 rows of ☐ = 16

C. Make your own puzzles.

Math Discoveries About Counting and Numbers, Grades 1-3 • © Ideal School Supply Company

Name _____

Use ▶ Number Tiles and a pencil.

✏️ ▶ Record your work.

A. Use number tiles 1 through 18.

Put the tiles in rows of three.
Keep the numbers in order.

Show how many tiles you use for the rows.

1 row of 3 = ☐

2 rows of 3 = ☐

3 rows of 3 = ☐

4 rows of 3 = ☐

5 rows of 3 = ☐

6 rows of 3 = ☐

B. Use the same number tiles.

Solve these puzzles.

3 rows of ☐ = 18   2 rows of ☐ = 18

C. Make your own puzzles.

29

Use ▶ Number Tiles and a pencil.

 Record your work.

A. Use number tiles 1 through 24.

Put the tiles in rows of six.
Keep the numbers in order.

Show how many tiles you use for the rows.

1 row of 6 = ☐

2 rows of 6 = ☐

3 rows of 6 = ☐

4 rows of 6 = ☐

B. Use the same number tiles.

Solve these puzzles.

3 rows of ☐ = 24   2 rows of ☐ = 24

C. Make your own puzzles.

30

Use ▶ Number Tiles and a pencil.

 Record your work.

A. Use number tiles 1 through 30.

Put the tiles in rows of five.
Keep the numbers in order.

Show how many tiles you use for the rows.

1 row of 5 = ☐

2 rows of 5 = ☐

3 rows of 5 = ☐

4 rows of 5 = ☐

5 rows of 5 = ☐

6 rows of 5 = ☐

B. Use the same number tiles.

Solve these puzzles.

3 rows of ☐ = 30   5 rows of ☐ = 30

C. Make your own puzzles.

Name _____

Use ▶ Number Line and a pencil.

 ▶ Record your work.

Find the rule for each robot.
Fill in the missing numbers.

A.

Number In	Number Out
3	5
2	4
7	9
4	6
8	
5	

Robot's Rule?   Number In = Number Out

B.

Number In	Number Out
5	10
7	12
8	13
6	11
10	
14	

Robot's Rule?   Number In = Number Out

C. Write and draw your own robot puzzle.

Use ▶ Number Line and a pencil.

 Record your work.

Find the rule for each robot.
Fill in the missing numbers.

A.

Number In	Number Out
9	6
7	4
8	5
4	1
10	
12	

Robot's Rule?   Number In $\bigcirc$ $-$ $\square$ = Number Out

B.

Number In	Number Out
20	15
10	5
18	13
11	6
9	
12	

Robot's Rule?   Number In $\bigcirc$ $-$ $\square$ = Number Out

C. Write and draw your own robot puzzle.

Find the rule for each robot.
Fill in the missing numbers.

A.

Number In	Number Out
2	4
4	8
3	6
1	2
5	
6	

Robot's Rule?   Number In = Number Out

B.

Number In	Number Out
1	3
3	9
4	12
5	15
2	
7	

Robot's Rule?   Number In = Number Out

C. Write and draw your own robot puzzle.

Name _____

Use ▶ Number Line and a pencil.

✏️ ▶ Record your work.

Find the rule for each robot.
Fill in the missing numbers and signs.

A.

Number In	Number Out
16	8
12	4
15	7
10	2
18	
24	

Robot's Rule?   Number In ◯ ▢ = Number Out

B.

Number In	Number Out
4	12
6	18
7	21
5	15
8	
3	

Robot's Rule?   Number In ◯ ▢  = Number Out

C. Write and draw your own robot puzzle.

Name

Use ▶ Number Line and a pencil.

✏ ⬭ Record your work.

35

Find the rule for each robot.
Fill in the missing numbers and signs.

A.

Number In	Number Out
7	17
4	14
1	11
10	20
12	
9	
18	

Robot's Rule?　　Number In ◯ ▢ = Number Out

B.

Number In	Number Out
50	30
35	15
60	40
43	23
61	
75	
59	

Robot's Rule?　　Number In ◯ ▢ = Number Out

C. Write and draw your own robot puzzle.

35

Name

Use▶ 1-100 Chart, Number Line, Number Tiles, and a pencil.

✏️▷ Record your work.

Solve the number puzzles.
Choose what to use.

A. Teresa has three dimes and one nickel.
What number tells how many pennies her
coins are worth.

B. Joel is thinking of a number.
It is an odd number between 40 and 50.
It is closer to 40 than to 50. What number could it be?

C. Where do you think the number 13 would be on this number line?
Mark the spot.

D. What numbers are missing?

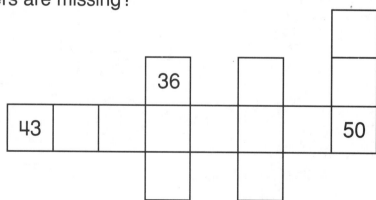

Math Discoveries About Counting and Numbers, Grades 1-3 • © Ideal School Supply Company

Name

Use ▶ 1-100 Chart, Number Line, Number Tiles, and a pencil.

Record your work.

Solve the number puzzles.
Choose what to use.

A. Jasmine and her older sister go to dance class 24 blocks from their home. They walk 3 blocks to the subway. They ride 18 blocks on the subway. They walk the rest of the way to dance class. How many blocks do they walk after their subway ride?

B. Where do you think the number 25 would be on this number line? Mark the spot.

C. What numbers are missing?

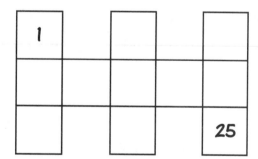

D. What could the mystery number be?

I am an even number.
I am between 30 and 50.
I am closer to 30 than to 50.

Name _____

Use ▶ 1-100 Chart, Number Line, Number Tiles, and a pencil.

 Record your work.

38

Solve the number puzzles.
Choose what to use.

A. Write the numbers in order from lowest to highest.
   What numbers come next?

   35, 20, 25, 30, 15

   _____, _____, _____, _____, _____, _____, _____, _____

B. What could these mystery numbers be?

   We are neighbors on the number chart.
   Two of us are even numbers.
   Two of us are odd numbers.
   In two of us, the tens' digit and ones' digit are the same.

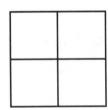

C. Is 33 closer to 25 or to 50?

D. Look at the steps.
   How many blocks will it take to make steps 6 blocks high?

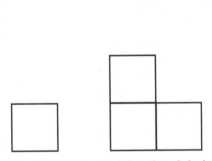

1 block high 2 blocks high

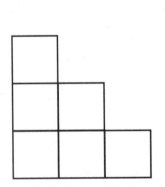

3 blocks high

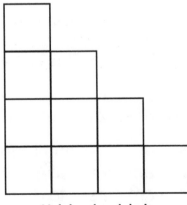

4 blocks high

39

Name

Use ▶ 1-100 Chart, Number Line, Number Tiles, and a pencil.

✏️ Record your work.

Solve the number puzzles.
Choose what to use.

A. The Mudds planted seeds in their garden. Zach put in 2 seeds, and 4 plants came up. Molly planted 5 seeds, and 10 plants came up. Holly planted 4 seeds, and 8 plants came up. What was happening in the Mudds' garden? If Jack plants 9 seeds, how many plants will come up?

B. Which numbers are equal? Connect them.

12 + 5	10 + 10 + 5
25 + 50	1 less than 50
89 – 40	100 – 25
50 – 25	7 more than 10

C. What could these mystery numbers be?

We are neighbors on the number chart.
We are greater than 25.
We are less than 75.
Each of us has 7 ones.

D. Is 80 closer to 50 or to 100?

Math Discoveries About Counting and Numbers, Grades 1-3 • © Ideal School Supply Company

Name _____

Use ▶ 1-100 Chart, Number Line, Number Tiles, and a pencil.

 Record your work.

Solve the number puzzles.
Choose what to use.

A. The third grade is going to
WaterLand! The boys and girls
pile into the bus. They fill 7 rows
of seats. There are 4 seats in
every row. How many third-
graders are on the bus?

B. Which number is closest to 100?

17 + 80

48 + 51

25 more than 72

40 more than 58

C. What number is half of 100?

D. What numbers between 1 and 100 have a 5 in them?

Name(s)_____

Take number tiles 0 through 25.
Put them in a paper bag and shake them.

Work with a partner.

Take turns.
On your turn, take a handful of number tiles out of the bag.
Put the number tiles in order.

Ask your partner to use a number line to check.

Name(s)_____

Work with a partner.

Use a number line.
Write clues about mystery numbers.

Let friends find your mystery numbers.

Extension for Activities 11-15

Name(s) _____

Work with a partner.

Use a number line.
Write number puzzles.
Write number sentences to match.

Start at: _____   Start at: _____

Count on: _____   Count back: _____

End number? _____   End number? _____

☐ + ☐ = ☐   ☐ – ☐ = ☐

Ask a friend to solve your puzzles and fill in the number sentences.

- -

Extension for Activities 16-20

Name(s) _____

Work with a partner.

Use two small beans and a 1-100 chart.

1-100									
1	2	3	4	5	6	7	8	9	10
11	12	13	14	15	16	17	18	19	20
21	22	23	24	25	26	27	28	29	30

Take turns.
On your turn, put the beans on two numbers on the chart.
Show which is the start number and which is the end number.
How fast can your partner tell how much you counted on or counted back?

How did you find the answers quickly? Talk about this together.

Math Discoveries About Counting and Numbers, Grades 1-3 • © Ideal School Supply Company

Name(s) _____

Work with a partner.

Use a 0-99 chart or a 1-100 chart.
Write clues about mystery numbers.

Show your clues to other pairs of partners.
Can they find your mystery numbers?

Name(s) _____

There are only two ways to make even rows with 2, 3, and 5 tiles:

Number of Tiles	Way 1	Way 2
2	1 row of 2	2 rows of 1
3	1 row of 3	3 rows of 1
5	1 row of 5	5 rows of 1

What are some other numbers that make even rows in only two ways?
Work with a partner. Use number tiles to find out. Record.

Show your work to another pair of partners.
Talk about what you discovered.

Extension for Activities 31-35

Work with a partner.

Draw and write a Robot's Rule puzzle.

Exchange puzzles with another pair of partners.
Solve the puzzles. Then talk about how you solved them.

- -

Extension for Activities 36-40

Name(s)

Work with a partner.

Use number tiles, number charts, and a number line.

Write puzzles about numbers.
You can use stories and drawings in your puzzles.

Let another pair of partners solve your puzzles.
Ask them to tell you what they are thinking while they solve the puzzles.

Number Lines Around Us

Description: Students look around the classroom for lines of numbers, and draw the objects on which they find them. The students organize and display their objects in a chart or graph, and tell how the lines of numbers are used. Next, the children look for other lines of numbers outside of the classroom. They draw or cut out pictures of the objects on which they find the numbers, and bring them to school. Groups of students organize the pictures and display them on a bulletin board.

Skills Developed: Students develop an awareness of the many items they use in their daily lives that have numbers lined up in order on them. As the children investigate how they use the lines of numbers, they become aware of relationships between numbers, and between numbers and measurement. They collect data, sort and classify and organize it, and display their results.

Getting Ready: Have a small group of students work in pairs. Give each pair of students a pencil, paper, and a number line.

Finding Lines of Numbers

Have the children look at their number lines. Say: **Think about how you used this line of numbers.** Give the children a few moments, then let them share their ideas about how they used the line of numbers.

Tell the children that you would like to have them look around the classroom and try to find things that have lines of numbers on them. Tell them that the numbers can be in a straight line or in a curved line. Give the children about 10 minutes to search for the items in the classroom. Ask them to

draw each item they find. (The children may discover such items as a ruler, clock, yardstick, scale, thermometer, television dial.) After each pair of students has found at least one item, ask the children to return to the group and tell about their discoveries. Help them compare the lines of numbers and talk about how they are alike and different. Ask them to tell how they would use the lines of numbers on the items.

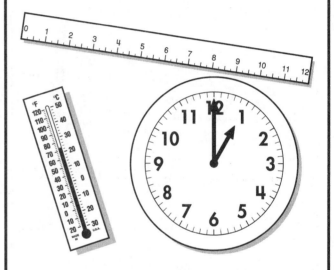

Then have the children sort the items into groups and decide how to display the groups on a bulletin board.

More Lines of Numbers

Ask the students: **How many more lines of numbers can you find outside of our classroom?** Have the children try to estimate how many more things they can find that have lines of numbers on them. Then give the children pencils and paper and explain that you want them to draw a picture of every thing they find and write a few words describing how a person would use the numbers on it. You might want to suggest that students ask their families to help them search for the numbers.

Have the students write a letter to someone, showing pictures of two of the things they found in the classroom, and asking that person for help in finding more. You may want to suggest that the children show examples of a straight line and a curved line of numbers. Let the students talk together about what they want to show and say in their letters. Here is one example:

Dear _____

We are using a number line in school to learn about numbers. The numbers are lined up in order on the number line. We found other lines of numbers on things in our classroom. Here are two things we found:

I want to find more things that have lines of numbers on them. Will you please help me?

Thank you for your help.

_____

Have the children deliver their letters and collect their information.

When two or more pairs of students bring in their information, let them meet as a group and share what they discovered. Encourage them to compare

the lines of numbers they found and talk about how they are alike and different. How were the numbers used? How important were the numbers? Were any of them important for their safety?

Let the children decide how they would like to organize and display their information on a bulletin board. They may want to sort the items into groups based on how the numbers are arranged, or on how the numbers are used, or on a different plan for grouping. One example is given below.

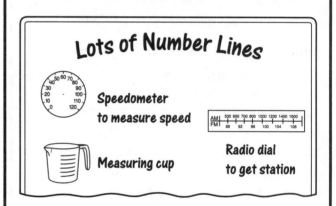

Lots of Number Lines

Speedometer
to measure speed

Measuring cup

Radio dial
to get station

Investigation 2

Create a Calendar

Description: Students talk about how a calendar and a number chart are alike and how they are different. Then pairs of students write a story about a land in which the calendar is different from their own calendar. They choose the number of days in a week, weeks in a month, and months in a year for their story land. They figure out how old they would be if they lived in their story land. Finally, they display their new calendar and their story for other students to enjoy.

Skills Developed: Students use their imaginations, creativity, language skills, and math skills to write a story. They develop a greater understanding of the use of numbers in calendars and in time-related aspects of their own lives. The students also develop their ability to communicate as they display their work for other children to see.

Getting Ready: Have a small group of students work in pairs. Provide a pencil, crayons or colored markers, and blank paper for each pair. Have a calendar and a 1-100 chart available for the group to use.

Calendar and Number Chart

Ask the students to look at the calendar and at the 1-100 chart and think about how they are alike and different. Let the students express their ideas about the similarities and differences. They may notice that the numbers are in order on the calendar like they are on the number chart. They may notice that the numbers only go as high as 31 on a calendar, whereas they continue on to 100 on the number chart. They may also notice that the numbers are shown in rows of 10 on the number chart, but in rows of 7 on the calendar. They may notice

too that every space is filled in each row of the number chart, but not all spaces are filled in the rows of the calendar. Let the children talk about the reasons for the differences they see between the chart and the calendar.

Ask the students about how they use the numbers on calendars. What do the numbers tell them? Why are there seven spaces in every row on the calendar? Why do some months have numbers 1 through 31, and some months have fewer numbers? How many months are there in a year? How many days do they have to wait until their next birthday?

When the students have finished comparing the chart and calendar, give each pair a pencil, blank paper, and crayons or markers. Tell them that you would like to have them make up a story about some animals or children in a land where the calendar is different from their own. The characters in the story are waiting for their birthdays to come, because they are going to have a wonderful party. Tell the students to decide what the calendar looks like in this imaginary land. How many days are there are in a week? How many days are there in a month? How many months are there in a year? What picture would be a good illustration for each month of the year? Have each pair of students make their own calendar, including illustrations, and write their story.

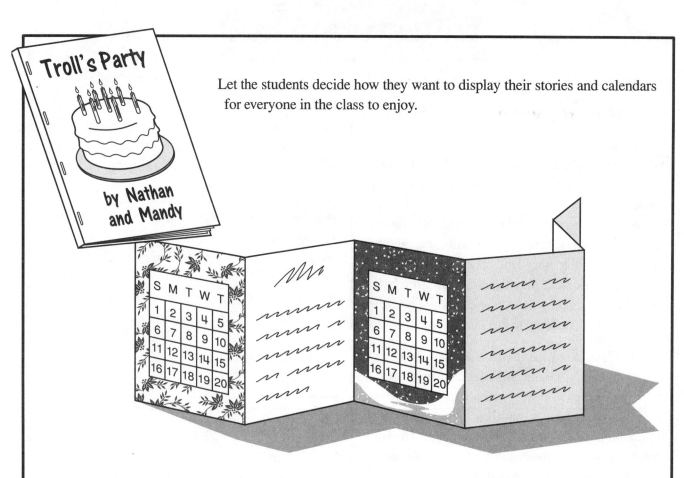

Let the students decide how they want to display their stories and calendars for everyone in the class to enjoy.

How Old Are You in Story Land?

Ask each pair of students to figure out how old they would be if they lived in their story land. Provide calculators for the students to use.

When two or three pairs of students have computed their ages in the imaginary lands, let them meet and compare their ages. Encourage them to talk about how their ages are related to the number of days in the year shown on their calendars.

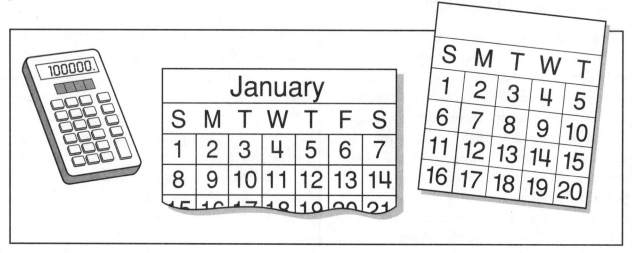

Trail Twister

READY   You will need the Trail Twister game cards and a 1-100 chart.

You will need two crayons or markers in different colors.

SET   Shuffle the game cards. Give two cards to each player.
Put the rest of the cards face down on a draw pile.

Each take a crayon or marker.

The player who has the shorter first name begins the game.

PLAY   To win, you must be the first player to have a trail of connected
numbers from the first row of the chart to the last row.
Connected numbers share sides.

Take turns. On your first turn, choose number 1, 2, 3, 4, 5, 6, 7,
8, 9, or 10. Use your color to mark the number on the chart.
Players must choose different numbers.

On other turns, choose one of your cards. Do what the card tells
you. Mark the number. Put your card face down under the draw
pile. Draw a new card.

Players may not share numbers.

The first player to have a trail of connected numbers from the
first row of the chart to the last row is the winner.

**PLAY IT
AGAIN**   Make your own cards.

Trail Twister	**Trail Twister**	**Trail Twister**	**Trail Twister**
Start on one of your numbers. Count on 1.	Start on one of your numbers. Count on 9.	Start on one of your numbers. Count on 10.	Start on one of your numbers. Count on 11.
Trail Twister	**Trail Twister**	**Trail Twister**	**Trail Twister**
Start on one of your numbers. Count on 10.	Start on one of your numbers. Count on 9.	Start on one of your numbers. Count back 10.	Start on one of your numbers. Count back 11.
Trail Twister	**Trail Twister**	**Trail Twister**	**Trail Twister**
Find an even number less than 20.	Find an odd number between 20 and 30.	Find an even number between 31 and 41.	Find an odd number between 40 and 50.
Trail Twister	**Trail Twister**	**Trail Twister**	**Trail Twister**
Find an even number between 51 and 71.	Find an odd number greater than 50.	Find an even number less than 79.	Find an odd number between 80 and 100.
Trail Twister	**Trail Twister**	**Trail Twister**	**Trail Twister**
Find a number that has 9 in it.	Find a number that has 3 in it.	Find a number that has 5 in it. Take another turn.	Find a number that has 8 in it. Take another turn.